The Official Countdown to the London 2012 Games

Simon Hart

Are you ready to go Mandeville?

You bet Wenlock. Let's discover the London 2012 Games!

CARLTON

The Games are coming!

On 27 July 2012, a flame will be lit in the Olympic Stadium in London. It will mark the start of the world's biggest sporting event. Nearly 15,000 athletes will take part in the London 2012 Olympic Games and Paralympic Games. Millions of people will buy tickets to the Games and billions more will watch them on TV.

Winning the Games

London took part in a competition with Moscow, New York, Madrid and Paris for the chance to host the 2012 Olympic Games and Paralympic Games. On 6 July 2005, the people in charge of the Olympic Games voted for their favourite city. Afterwards, the president of the International Olympic Committee, Jacques Rogge, opened an envelope and read out the name of the winning city – it was London!

A crowd of 30,000 people gathered in Trafalgar Square in London to find out who would host the 2012 Games. As the result was announced, there was a huge roar of delight and people cheered and waved flags. There were similar celebrations all around the country. The party had begun!

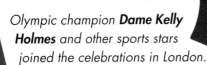

*Olympic champion **Dame Kelly Holmes** and other sports stars joined the celebrations in London.*

4

Close call

Many people thought Paris would win the vote to host the 2012 Games. During the early rounds of voting, New York, Moscow and Madrid were knocked out, leaving just Paris and London left. The final round was extremely close, but London came out on top, winning by just four votes!

*The Olympic flag was handed to the **Mayor of London** at the close of the Beijing 2008 Games to show that London was now the next host city.*

A boost for sport

Double Olympic gold medallist, Sebastian Coe, the leader of the London bid, said that he wanted the 2012 Games to encourage young people to play sport. To show the importance of children, a group of 30 young people from east London were chosen to travel to Singapore for the vote.

Superstar supporters

Football superstar David Beckham was among the famous people who travelled to Singapore to support London's bid to host the Games. David grew up in east London, near to the site of the new Olympic Stadium.

*World famous footballer **David Beckham** and Olympic Athletics gold medal-winner **Denise Lewis** are all smiles in Singapore after London's winning bid.*

*The president of the International Olympic Committee congratulates **Sebastian Coe** (right).*

The Olympic and Paralympic Games

The Olympic Games are the oldest, largest and greatest sporting competition on the planet. Together with the Paralympic Games for athletes with a disability, they are a spectacular celebration of the world's greatest sportsmen and sportswomen.

The Summer Olympic and Paralympic Games are held every four years in a different host city. In London, athletes will compete in 26 Olympic sports and 20 Paralympic sports. The prize for winning is something that every athlete dreams of – an Olympic or Paralympic gold medal!

Only a few hundred athletes took part in the first modern Olympic Games in Athens in 1896. Since then, the Games have grown enormously. The Olympic Games in London will involve 10,500 men and women from 205 countries. A further 4,200 athletes will take part in the Paralympic Games.

The Olympic Games last for 17 days. In 2012, they will take place from 27 July until 12 August. The Paralympic Games last for 11 days, from 29 August until 9 September. Most events will be held in London, but some will take place in different parts of the country.

Excitement will build and build until the Olympic Flame is lit and the London 2012 Games officially begin!

A world united

The symbol of the Olympic Games is five interconnected rings. These stand for the five regions of the world that come together for the Games: Africa, Asia, the Americas, Europe and Oceania.

The Opening Ceremony

The Olympic Games and Paralympic Games begin with spectacular Opening Ceremonies where a flame is lit in the Olympic Stadium. This burns right until the end of the Games. For the Olympic Games, the fire used to light the flame comes from Olympia in Greece, where the ancient Games took place. The flame is then passed from one runner to another, all the way to the Olympic Stadium. This is called the Torch Relay.

The Paralympic Games

The 'Para' in Paralympic Games is short for 'parallel'. It means that they run alongside the Olympic Games.

4.7 billion TV viewers watched the Beijing 2008 Olympic Games and Paralympic Games. That's nearly three out of every four people in the entire world!

A colourful part of the Opening Ceremony is the athletes' parade. All the nations taking part in the Games march through the Olympic Stadium with their flags.

Meet the mascots!

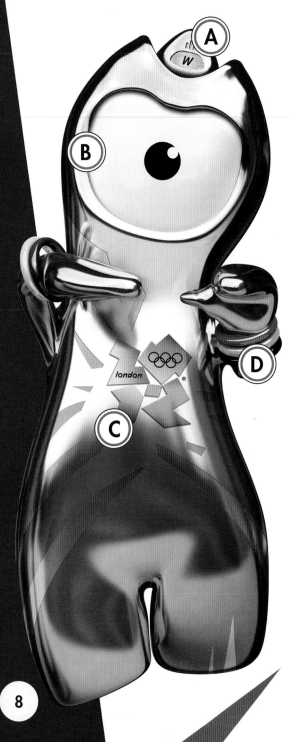

Meet Wenlock and Mandeville, the mascots of the 2012 Games. They are keen to help children learn about Olympic and Paralympic sports and the history of the Games.

The story of the mascots

Michael Morpurgo, a famous children's author, has written a story about Wenlock and Mandeville. It tells how they were made from the last two drops of steel used to build the Olympic Stadium. A rainbow magically brings the mascots to life and they set off to discover everything they can about the Games!

Wenlock is the Olympic Games mascot, named after the English town of Much Wenlock. More than 150 years ago, this town held sporting competitions and gave Baron Pierre de Coubertin the idea for starting the modern Olympic Games in 1896.

(A) **Headlight:** inspired by the yellow lights on London's iconic black taxis

(B) **Camera lens:** this lets Wenlock record everything at London 2012

(C) **London 2012 logo:** shows how the Games are close to Wenlock's heart

(D) **Friendship bands:** the five Olympic rings are a symbol of friendship between nations

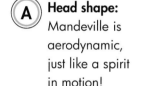

mandeville

Mandeville is the Paralympic Games mascot, named after an English town called Stoke Mandeville. In 1948 a doctor at the town's hospital organised a sporting competition for injured soldiers. This led to the creation of the Paralympic Games.

Catch Wenlock and Mandeville

The story of Wenlock and Mandeville continues. In the run-up to the London 2012 Games, the two mascots are travelling all over the United Kingdom, trying out lots of Olympic and Paralympic sports. Spot them in your local area, or follow their adventures online at: **mylondon2012.com/mascots**

A **Head shape:** Mandeville is aerodynamic, just like a spirit in motion!

B **Camera lens:** to capture every moment of the Paralympic Games

C **Streamlined body:** Mandeville's shape helps quick movements

D **Wrist timer:** Lets Mandeville keep track of progress

Start the Countdown!

Join Wenlock and Mandeville on a journey through time as they discover the history of the Olympic Games and Paralympic Games. Follow the timeline all the way to the London 2012 Games!

Get ready, set... go!

The Games begin

The Olympic Games go right back to ancient Greece!

The Olympic Games were first held in about 776 BC at a place called Olympia in ancient Greece. They were part of a religious festival to honour Zeus, the king of the Greek gods. The Games were then held every four years for more than 1,000 years.

Greek athletes ran races at the original Games without running shoes – or any clothes!

The first Olympic Games

In the first Olympic Games there was only one event, called the Stade. It was a running race over about 190 metres from one end of the stadium to the other. Later, other events were added to the Games, such as Boxing, Wrestling, Javelin, Discus and Chariot racing.

Only men could take part in the original Olympic Games. Unmarried girls were allowed to watch, but if a married woman sneaked into the Games she could be thrown off a cliff!

The last ancient Olympic Games were held in 393 AD. By that time, Greece was ruled by the Romans. Theodosius, the Roman emperor, disliked the Games and decided to end them.

The modern Games

In the 1880s, a French nobleman called Baron Pierre de Coubertin had the idea of starting the Olympic Games up again. His plan was to hold a sporting competition between athletes from different countries that would be similar to the ancient Games. Not everyone liked his idea at first, but he refused to give up. Finally, his dream came true and the modern Olympic Games were born.

Pierre de Coubertin hoped the Games would bring nations closer together.

776 BC
The first ever Olympic Games were held! The first known Olympic champion was a cook called Koroibos who won the Stade.

Athens 1896

The first modern Games were held in 1896 in Athens, the capital of Greece. They were much smaller than the Olympic Games are now. Only 241 athletes from 14 countries took part. All of them were men, because women were still not allowed to compete.

Marathon man

The hero of the 1896 Games was a 24-year-old shepherd called Spyridon Louis, who won the Marathon, a 40-kilometre running race. There were 100,000 spectators at the stadium in Athens to cheer his victory.

The Olympic Flame that starts the Games today is based on an ancient Greek myth about fire being stolen from Zeus.

Eyes on the prize
What did a winner at the ancient Olympic Games get instead of a gold medal?

 ○ **Silver** crown

 ○ **Olive** branch

 ○ **Laurel** wreath

Answer on page 95.

1896
On 6 April the first modern Olympic Games opened in Athens, Greece, in front of 60,000 spectators.

London's Games

In 2012, London will become the first city in the world to have hosted the Olympic Games three times. The Games were held in London in 1908 and 1948, but these were very different from the massive sporting event of today.

The London 1908 Olympic Games were much bigger than earlier Games, but there were just 2,008 competitors from 22 countries. Most of the events took place in a stadium called White City in west London, where the swimming pool was actually inside the running track!

The Marathon was made longer to give the Royal Family the best view.

The race began at Windsor Castle and finished in front of the Royal Box inside the stadium. The course was measured at 26 miles, 385 yards and became the official distance for the Marathon.

The most famous incident of the 1908 Games happened in the Marathon. The Italian runner Dorando Pietri was in the lead, but when he entered the stadium he was so exhausted that he collapsed five times. Some people helped him over the finish line, but this was against the rules, so poor Pietri was disqualified.

Dorando Pietri lost the gold medal, but Queen Alexandra gave him a cup to reward his courage.

1896

US athlete James Connolly became the first modern Olympic champion, winning the Triple jump.

London 1948

The Olympic Games were supposed to take place in London in 1944, but they had to be cancelled because of the Second World War. Instead, the Games took place in London in 1948. They were the first Olympic Games to be held for 12 years. About 4,000 athletes from 59 countries took part. There was very little money to spare after the war, so competitors were even asked to bring their own food!

The flying Dutchwoman

The star of the 1948 Games was a Dutch woman called Fanny Blankers-Koen, who won four gold medals in sprint races. She was nicknamed the Flying Housewife!

Odd one out
Which of these sports was NOT part of the 1908 Olympic Games?

◯ **Motor Boating**

◯ **Basketball**

◯ **Rugby**

Answer on page 95.

1896
John Boland won gold for Tennis, but only took part in the Games because he was on holiday in Athens at the same time!

Greatest moments

There have been many extraordinary moments at the Olympic Games and Paralympic Games. Moments of triumph and joy, but also some disappointments. Here are some of the most memorable.

Paris 1924

Paavo Nurmi, a runner from Finland, won the 1,500 metres and 5,000m finals with just 26 minutes of rest between. He won an amazing nine gold medals between 1920 and 1928.

Helsinki 1952

Czech athlete Emil Zatopek won the 5,000 metres, 10,000m and the Marathon! He is the only runner ever to win all three long-distance running races.

Rome 1960

Ethiopian runner Abebe Bikila won gold in the Marathon, even though he ran in bare feet!

Mexico City 1968

American sprinters Tommie Smith and John Carlos wore black gloves and clenched their fists when they received their medals after the 200 metres final. They were protesting at the way black people were treated in America.

Mexico City 1968

American Bob Beamon produced one of the greatest Olympic performances in history when he won the Long jump with a leap of 8.90 metres. He broke the world record by an astounding 55 centimetres!

1900

Paris hosted the second Olympic Games. These were the first Games where women could compete in their own events.

Moscow 1980

British track athletes Steve Ovett and Sebastian Coe were involved in two thrilling duels. Coe was the favourite to win the 800 metres, but was devastated to lose the gold medal to Ovett. Six days later, Coe returned to win gold in the 1,500 metres, while Ovett finished third.

Seoul 1988

American diver Greg Louganis made a mistake with one of his dives and smacked his head on the diving board. Showing great courage, he carried on and returned a few days later to win gold in the final.

Atlanta 1996

Muhammad Ali, who won an Olympic gold medal for America in 1960 and went on to become a boxing superstar, had the honour of lighting the Olympic cauldron. It was an emotional moment because he was suffering from a brain disease and his body was shaking.

Sydney 2000

A crowd of 110,000 cheered as Australian athlete Louise Sauvage won the 800 metres wheelchair race. She won nine Paralympic gold medals during her racing career.

Beijing 2008

Chinese swimmer He Junquan amazed spectators by winning two gold medals and one silver, despite having no arms. He has won a total of seven gold medals in three Paralympic Games.

These amazing stories make me want to do my best too!

1904

Twelve countries travelled to St. Louis, USA, for the first Olympic Games to be held outside Europe.

Who's coming to London?

Over 200 countries will take part in the London 2012 Games. Here are the top 30 medal-winning countries from the 2008 Games.

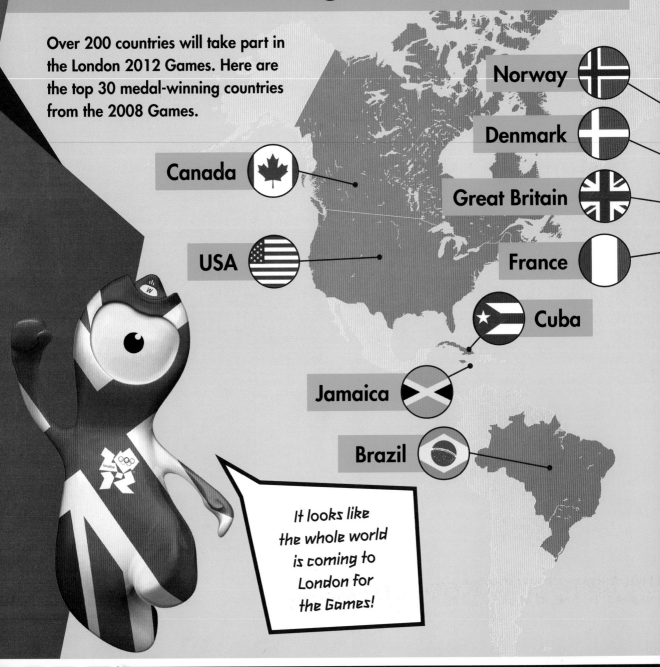

Norway

Denmark

Canada

Great Britain

USA

France

Cuba

Jamaica

Brazil

It looks like the whole world is coming to London for the Games!

1904

Fred Lorz's gold for the Marathon was taken away when it was discovered that he'd been driven part of the way in a car!

Netherlands

Belarus

Russia

Germany

Ukraine

Czech Republic

Kazakhstan

Poland

Slovakia

Italy

Hungary

Romania

Spain

Georgia

Japan

Ethiopia

South Korea

Kenya

China

Australia

New Zealand

1904

US gymnast George Eyser won six
Olympic medals, including one for rope
climbing, despite having a wooden leg.

17

Olympic buildings

The London 2012 Games will have world-class stadiums fit for the world's best athletes. Events will be held in a mixture of brand new and existing arenas in London and elsewhere in the United Kingdom. Most of the new venues are in an area of east London known as the Olympic Park. They include the 80,000-seat main Olympic Stadium, the Velodrome and the Aquatics Centre.

On track for gold

Cycling was Britain's most successful Olympic and Paralympic sport in 2008. At the London 2012 Games, Track Cycling will take place in a magnificent, new Velodrome inside the Olympic Park. The Velodrome has room for 6,000 spectators. Let's hope there will be plenty of British medal winners for them to cheer!

Next door to the Velodrome is the BMX Circuit, with its numerous bumps, jumps and steep-banked turns. It will have 6,000 temporary seats, which will be removed after the Games.

I'm going to be in the Stadium cheering everybody on!

18

1908

A volcanic eruption in Italy led to the Games being switched from Rome to London. These were the first London Olympic Games.

Making a splash

The new Aquatics Centre will be one of the most spectacular venues at the Games. Its roof is built in the shape of a wave. Inside there are two 50-metre swimming pools, a diving pool and seats for 17,500 spectators. It will be the venue for the Swimming and Diving competitions, while Water Polo will take place in a temporary arena next door.

The Olympic Stadium is the shining centrepiece of the Games. It will host the Opening and Closing Ceremonies as well as the Athletics events.

Just the ticket!

How many tickets will go on sale for the 2012 Games?

○ 10,000

○ 100,000

○ 10 million

Answer on page 95.

1908

British athletes won 56 gold medals. In fact, Britain won two more gold medals than the rest of the countries put together!

Olympic Village

During the Games, around 17,000 athletes and officials from around the world will live, eat and relax together in the Olympic Village. For many athletes, staying in the Village with other competitors is one of the highlights of the Games.

This place really is a home from home!

1908

Pierre de Coubertin wrote a message to all the athletes, saying that taking part in the Games was more important than winning.

Jonathan Edwards helped to design London's Olympic Village. He has competed at four Olympic Games, winning a gold medal in the Triple jump in 2000. Here, he answers questions about life in the Olympic Village.

Where will the athletes sleep during the Games?

They will stay in blocks of apartments in the Olympic Park, just a short walk from the main venues. Generally, six athletes will share an apartment. They will sleep in double rooms containing two single beds. Each country has its own section of the Village.

Where will they eat?

There will be one huge dining room, which will cater for about 5,000 people at a time. There will be a massive variety of food to choose from. One of the amazing things is that food will be served at all times of the day and night. And it is all completely free!

Will there be things to do in the Village?

For athletes who are not training or competing, there will be a cinema, a games area, an internet café, a gym, shops, even a hairdressing salon. The great thing about the Village is that it is also very close to a railway station, so athletes will find it easy to visit the sights of London.

Will Paralympic athletes use the same facilities as the Olympic athletes?

Absolutely. Everywhere in the Village will be fully accessible to athletes with disabilities.

What will happen to the Village after the Games?

The apartments will be redecorated and turned into new homes.

What would you say is the best thing about staying in an Olympic Village?

The feeling of being part of the world coming together in sport to celebrate what is best about human nature. With over 200 nations living together, there is an electric atmosphere inside the Village. There is nervousness about competing, but also great excitement about being part of the greatest show on earth.

1912

The Stockholm Games in Sweden were the first to welcome athletes from all five continents of the world.

The sustainable Games

The organisers of the Games want them to be 'sustainable', which means that they are protecting the environment and local wildlife as they get London ready for 2012. They also want to make improvements that last after the Games are over.

To reduce traffic and pollution, spectators will be able to travel to the Olympic Park in east London on high-speed trains from central London. This is called the Javelin® shuttle service and will carry up to 25,000 people every hour. There will also be lots of new paths so that fans can walk or cycle to the Games too. The organisers want everyone coming to the Games to leave their cars at home.

New walking and cycling routes provide a healthy and green way to travel to the Games.

In some previous host cities, the huge stadiums have been left empty and unused afterwards, which is very wasteful. In London, many of the buildings being used for sporting events are temporary. This means that when the Games are over, they can be taken down and used somewhere else.

Green power

A special energy centre will provide heating, cooling and electricity for the Olympic Park. Waste wood from the nearby area will help to power the energy centre. This will reduce the amount of carbon dioxide being produced, which is good for the planet.

Water features

More than 2,000 **newts** and over 100 **common toads** have been safely moved to new ponds and waterways. There are 8.35 kilometres of waterways in the Olympic Park area – that's about 167 lengths of a 50-metre pool!

1912
The high-tech Stockholm Games were the first to feature automatic timing equipment and photo finishes.

Say no to waste

Waste is being kept to a minimum for the 2012 Games. Rather than sending rubbish to a landfill site, the plan is to recycle and re-use wherever possible. When buildings had to be demolished to build the Olympic Park, nearly all of the bricks, stones and tiles were used again.

Animal friendly

Care has been taken to protect local wildlife as the Olympic Park is built. Children from a local school in east London are creating a nature reserve along the nearby River Lea. This will be home to many animals, such as birds, frogs, spiders and beetles. Some rare insects also live in the area, including the **Toadflax Brocade Moth**. New habitats will be created to make sure they have somewhere safe to live.

A green-fingered volunteer from a local school helps to improve the landscape around the Olympic Park.

Keep fit!

Sport is a very healthy thing to do. Organisers hope that the Olympic Games and Paralympic Games will set an example, encouraging more people to play sport and lead healthy lives.

Good for everyone

The plan is to make the 2012 Games accessible to everyone, not just as spectators, but also by providing jobs, training and opportunities for people to get involved.

1912
The wrestling semi-final between Russia's Martin Klein and Finland's Alfred Asikainen lasted for an incredible 11 hours!

Olympic sports

I want to try all these amazing Olympic sports!

Competitors will go for gold in 26 different Olympic sports at the 2012 Games. Here's the essential info on all these Olympic sports!

Aquatics – Diving

Athletes perform twists and somersaults off a three-metre springboard or a 10m platform. They can dive individually or in pairs.

Archery

Competitors shoot arrows at a target from a distance of 70 metres. The closer each arrow is to the target centre, the higher the score.

Aquatics – Swimming

Swimmers race in a pool using freestyle (crawl), breaststroke, butterfly or backstroke. Marathon races are held outside on open water.

Athletics

With 46 different events, including Track races for runners and Field events for throwers and jumpers, Athletics is the biggest Olympic sport.

Synchronised Swimming

A women-only sport in which athletes perform routines in the pool set to music. They compete in pairs or groups of eight.

Badminton

A racket game in which players try to hit a feather shuttlecock over a net to touch the ground on their opponents' side of the court.

Aquatics – Water Polo

A ball sport played in the pool. Teams of six outfield players and one goalkeeper try to score goals in their opponents' net.

Basketball

Teams of five players try to score by shooting the ball through their opponents' hoop, or basket. A match consists of four 10-minute quarters.

1920

After an eight-year break due to the First World War, the Belgian city of Antwerp hosted the Olympic Games.

Woah! So that's what they mean by white water!

Boxing

A combat sport for men and women who wear padded gloves and protective headgear. Points are scored by landing punches on an opponent.

Canoe Slalom

Canoeists race against the clock down a white-water course through up to 25 gates. Penalties are awarded for touching or missing a gate.

Canoe Sprint

Races for individuals or crews of up to four people are held on flat water over distances between 200 and 1,000 metres.

Cycling – BMX

Riders compete against each other in knockout rounds. They race on a short outdoor track that features plenty of jumps, bumps and corners.

Cycling – Mountain Bike

Races are about 40–50 kilometres for men and 30–40km for women. They take place over hilly countryside with trees, rocks and streams.

Cycling – Road

Men's Road Races are about 240 kilometres and women's about 130km. In the shorter Time Trial, riders race one by one against the clock.

Cycling – Track

Cyclists race around a banked, 250-metre track inside a velodrome. Long and short distance races are held for individuals and teams.

Equestrian – Dressage

Riders complete a Dressage test, guiding their horses through a series of special movements. Rider and horse are awarded marks by judges.

Equestrian – Eventing

A triple test for horse and rider. Held over four days, it includes a dressage test, a cross-country event and a jumping competition.

Equestrian – Jumping

Riders and their horses race against the clock over a course of fences, but are penalised for knocking fences down or for being too slow.

1920

The Antwerp Games attracted a record number of 2,626 athletes from countries as far away as New Zealand.

Fencing

A modern version of sword fighting using three types of weapon: Foil, Epée and Sabre. Competitors wear protective clothing and masks.

 ## Football

An 11-a-side ball game played by men and women in which the teams try to score goals in their opponents' net. Each match lasts for 90 minutes.

 ## Gymnastics – Artistic

A test of strength, skill and grace as male gymnasts compete on six types of equipment while women compete on four.

 ## Gymnastics – Rhythmic

A women-only sport. Gymnasts perform to music using a rope, hoop, ball, clubs or a long ribbon. Competitions are for individuals or teams of five.

 ## Gymnastics – Trampoline

Athletes perform twists and somersaults as they jump up and down on a trampoline. They can bounce higher than a two-storey house.

 ## Handball

A game played by teams of seven in which players use only their hands to move the ball or throw it into their opponents' net.

 ## Hockey

Teams of 11 use hockey sticks to move the ball and shoot it into their opponents' goal. Players hit the ball with the flat side of their hockey sticks.

Watch out, I'm going to take a shot at the goal!

 ## Judo

A martial art in which competitors use special throws or holds to defeat their opponent. Men and women fight in different weight classes.

Modern Pentathlon

Men and women compete in five different sports during a single day: Fencing, Swimming, Riding and a combined Running and Shooting event.

 ## Rowing

Rowers race in individual boats or in crews of up to eight rowers. They compete as lightweights or heavyweights over a 2,000-metre course.

1920
The official Olympic Flag with its five interlocking rings was raised at the Olympic Games for the first time.

Sailing

Athletes use the wind to make their boats or windsurfing boards go as fast as possible. Boats can be for one, two or three people.

Shooting

In Pistol and Rifle events, competitors fire bullets at a fixed target. In Shotgun competitions they shoot lead pellets at moving clay targets.

Table Tennis

Players use a small bat to hit a ball over a net and across a table. Men and women play as individuals or in pairs.

Taekwondo

A martial art in which athletes earn points for landing kicks on their opponent's body. They wear special protective padding and helmets.

Tennis

A game for individuals or pairs in which competitors use a racket to hit a ball over a net and inside the lines of the playing area, or court.

Triathlon

This gruelling combination of three sports starts with a 1,500-metre swim, followed by a 40-kilometre cycle ride and a final 10km run.

Volleyball

A ball game for teams of six in which the object is to get the ball over a high net without letting it touch the ground.

Volleyball – Beach

This has similar rules to standard Volleyball, but is played by teams of two on a smaller court that is covered in sand.

Weightlifting

Athletes compete to see who can lift the heaviest weights using two types of lift: the snatch and the clean and jerk.

Wrestling

Athletes grapple with each other to try to force their opponent's shoulders on to the ground. There are two Wrestling styles: Freestyle and Greco-Roman.

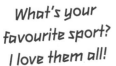

What's your favourite sport? I love them all!

Good luck Team GB!

British athletes hope to win lots of medals at the London 2012 Olympic Games. Great Britain's Olympic team are called Team GB. You can give them a boost at the London 2012 Games by cheering and waving your flag!

Team GB will have more than 500 athletes at the Olympic Games. It will be the largest British team for more than a century. Team GB is one of the most successful Olympic teams in the world. At the last Games in Beijing in 2008, Team GB finished fourth in the final medals table with 19 gold medals, 13 silver medals and 15 bronze medals. Can they win even more in London?

TEAM GB

Britain has taken part in every Olympic Games since the Games in Athens in 1896. The biggest ever British team was at the 1908 London Games, when 676 British athletes competed. The smallest was at St Louis, in America, in 1904. Britain had just three team members, but they still managed to win one gold and one silver medal.

Some Team GB athletes who will take part in the 2012 Games have already won lots of Olympic gold medals. Cyclist Sir Chris Hoy has won four gold medals and is one of the most successful British Olympic athletes of all time. Bradley Wiggins, who is also a cyclist, and sailor Ben Ainslie have both won three gold medals.

Flying the flag

One lucky Team GB member will have the honour of carrying the UK's flag at the Opening Ceremony. The athlete is usually chosen in a vote by their team mates.

1920

At the Opening Ceremony in Antwerp, Belgian athlete Victor Boin took an oath to play fair on behalf of all the athletes.

Leader of the track

Sebastian Coe, the head of the London 2012 Games, was a very successful Olympic track athlete. He won two gold medals and two silver medals at the 1980 and 1984 Olympic Games.

Pure gold

Dame Kelly Holmes and Rebecca Adlington are among Britain's most successful female athletes. Kelly won two gold medals at the 2004 Athens Games in Track Athletics. Rebecca won two Swimming gold medals in Beijing in 2008. She is hoping to win even more gold medals at the London 2012 Games.

The British women's Hockey team celebrate scoring a goal.

Come on Team GB! We are all right behind you!

Home run

Athletes competing in their home country often have an advantage over their opponents because they have a home crowd to cheer them on. It is very common for the host country to win more medals than they usually do at the Olympic Games. If you are lucky enough to get a ticket to the Games, remember to cheer for the British athletes.

1920

The Antwerp Olympic Games were the first where doves were released as a symbol of peace during the Opening Ceremony.

Aquatics

Aquatics is made up of four water sports: Swimming, Diving, Synchronised Swimming and Water Polo. Split-second finishes make Swimming one of the most exciting Olympic sports, so the poolside is always packed with spectators!

The lowdown

What? Swimming races range from 50 metres to 10 kilometres. Swimmers use four strokes: freestyle (or crawl), breaststroke, backstroke and butterfly. Diving is a spectacular sport as athletes perform amazing somersaults and twists. Water Polo is a team ball sport. Synchronised Swimming events are only open to women.
Where? Aquatics Centre and in Hyde Park for Marathon Swimming races on open water.
Don't miss: Women's 800 metres freestyle.

Synchronised swimming is so graceful it is also known as water ballet!

Believe it or not

At the 1948 Games in London, American swimmer Allen Stack snapped a cord in his trunks and they started to fall down just before the start of the 100 metres backstroke final. Luckily, the race was delayed to let him change into a new pair of trunks and he went on to win the gold medal.

Jargon buster

MEDLEY: a swimming race in which an individual athlete or a relay team must swim separate lengths of backstroke, breaststroke, butterfly and freestyle.

Know the rule

Synchronised swimmers are not allowed to touch the bottom of the pool. If they do, they receive a two-point penalty!

1924

The Olympic Games returned to Paris. The Games were held in a brand new stadium and swimming pool complex.

Rebecca Adlington

REBECCA became the first British swimmer in 100 years to win two Olympic gold medals at the Beijing 2008 Games. She started swimming when she was six at her local pool in Mansfield, called the Sherwood Baths. After her outstanding Olympic achievement, the pool was renamed the Rebecca Adlington Swimming Centre in her honour. When she returned from Beijing, Rebecca was presented with a pair of golden shoes by the mayor of Mansfield!

Key Facts
Born: 17 February 1989
Height: 1.79m
Weight: 71kg
Home town: Mansfield
Event: 400 metres freestyle, 800m freestyle, 4 x 200m freestyle relay

Track Record
2008 Olympic Games in Beijing:
- Gold medal in 400m freestyle
- Gold medal in 800m freestyle
- World record of 8 minutes 14.10 seconds in 800m freestyle

Rebecca Adlington celebrates winning the women's 800m freestyle at the 2008 Games.

Thanks for the swimming tips Rebecca!

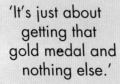

'It's just about getting that gold medal and nothing else.'

Different strokes
Name three Olympic swimming strokes that begin with B.

B _____

B _____

B _____

Answer on page 95.

1924
Finland's greatest long-distance runner, Paavo Nurmi, won an amazing five gold medals!

Athletics – Track

Athletics is the oldest Olympic sport, dating back to ancient Greece. Nowadays it is also the biggest. Track events are very easy to understand. Athletes compete in running or walking races to see who is the fastest!

The lowdown

What? Races can be as short as 100 metres or as long as 50 kilometres. In hurdles and steeplechase races, athletes must also jump over obstacles.

Where? The Olympic Stadium. The Marathon and walking races take place on roads.

Don't miss: Men's 100 metres final.

Believe it or not

At the 1932 Olympic Games in Los Angeles, runners in the 3,000 metres steeplechase had to run an extra 400 metres. The race official lost count of the number of laps!

Jargon buster

HEAT: a qualifying race where the top finishers go through to the next round and the slower athletes are knocked out.

I'm up to speed on Athletics now!

Know the rule

Races begin when the starting pistol is fired. If the gun is fired a second time, it means someone has set off too early. This is a false start. The guilty athlete is disqualified and the race starts again.

Usain Bolt, the world's faste[st] man, sprints to the finish lin[e]

1928

Britain's Harold Abrahams won the 100 metres gold, while team-mate Eric Liddell won gold in the 400 metres.

Mo Farah

MO was born in Somalia, in Africa, but has lived in London since he was eight. He is a long-distance runner who competes in the 5,000 and 10,000 metres. In 2010, he became the first UK athlete to win gold medals in both events at the European Championships. Long-distance runners like Mo have to train very hard to be the best. He spends a lot of his time training in Africa with the world's top athletes.

'I can definitely win a medal at the London Olympics.'

Mo has set his sights on winning an Olympic medal in his home city.

Key Facts
Born: 23 March 1983
Height: 1.71m
Weight: 64kg
Home town: London
Event: 5,000 and 10,000 metres

Track Record
2006: Silver medal in 5,000 metres at the European Championships in Gothenburg
2009: Gold medal in 3,000 metres at the European Indoor Championships in Turin
2010: Gold medals in 5,000 and 10,000 metres at the European Championships in Barcelona

Go the distance
Tick the box for each distance to show which type of race it is.

	Sprint	Long distance	Middle distance
1,500m	☐	☐	☐
10,000m	☐	☐	☐
400m	☐	☐	☐

Answer on page 95.

1928
The Olympic Flame was lit for the first time to mark the start of the Amsterdam Olympic Games.

Athletics – Field

Jumping and throwing are called field events because they take place on a field inside the running track. Athletes compete to see who can jump the highest or the longest and who can throw the furthest.

The lowdown

What? There are four jumping events. In the Long jump and Triple jump, athletes leap into a sandpit. In the High jump and Pole vault, they try to jump over a bar onto a mattress. The throwing events are the Discus, Hammer, Javelin and Shot put.
Where? Olympic Stadium.
Don't miss: Men's Triple jump.

Believe it or not

Dora Ratjen competed for Germany in the women's High Jump at the 1936 Olympics in Berlin. But she was actually a man in disguise! The high jumper's real name was Hermann Ratjen.

Jargon buster

FOSBURY FLOP: a style of high-jumping where the athlete jumps over the bar backwards and head first. It was named after its American inventor, Dick Fosbury.

Know the rule

In the Long jump and Triple jump, athletes must take off from behind a take-off board. If the jumper's take-off foot goes beyond the board, the jump is not counted.

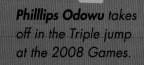

Phillips Odowu takes off in the Triple jump at the 2008 Games.

 # 1928

Greece led the parade at the Opening Ceremony while the host nation marched in last, starting a new Olympic tradition.

Jessica Ennis

Right, let's see how far I can throw this javelin!

JESSICA ENNIS is one of the UK's best hopes for an Olympic gold medal. She competes in the Heptathlon, a combination of seven track and field events that includes the 100 metres hurdles, 200m and 800m races, plus the High jump, Shot put, Long jump and Javelin. The winner can truly call herself the best all-round athlete. Jessica's best events are the 100m hurdles and the High jump. She can actually jump 30cm higher than her own height!

Key Facts

Born: 28 January 1986
Height: 1.65m
Weight: 57kg

Home town: Sheffield
Event: Heptathlon

Track Record

2009: Gold medal in Heptathlon at the World Championships in Berlin
2010: Gold medal in Pentathlon at the World Indoor Championships, Doha
2010: Gold medal in Heptathlon at the European Championships held in Barcelona

Jump to it!

Tick the number of hurdles you have to jump in a 100m hurdles race.

○ ○ ○

| 8 | 10 | 12 |

Jessica Ennis holds the Union Jack high and enjoys her moment of glory.

SPAR
1
BARCELONA 2010

'I want to make sure I grab my opportunity with both hands.'

Answer on page 95.

1928

Crown Prince Olav of Norway won a gold medal in Sailing. He was the first of four future kings to compete at the Games.

Basketball

I've got the hang of dribbling. Now to score!

Basketball is a fast-moving ball sport that is very popular with fans. Since men's Basketball became an Olympic sport in 1936, America has won gold 13 times out of 17. Women's Olympic Basketball started in 1976 and America has won gold six times out of nine.

The lowdown

What? Basketball is played on an indoor court by two teams of five players. The aim is to score points by shooting the ball into a net, or 'basket'. Players move the ball by passing it to each other or by running while bouncing the ball. The game consists of four 10-minute periods.
Where? Basketball Arena and North Greenwich Arena.
Don't miss: Men's final.

Believe it or not

Height gives Basketball players an advantage. The tallest player in modern Basketball is Yao Ming, of China, who is 2.29 metres tall!

Jargon buster

SLAM DUNK: when a player jumps up to the basket and slams the ball downwards into the net with one or both hands.

Know the rule

Players are not allowed to hold the ball or use two hands while running. Instead, they must 'dribble' the ball, bouncing it with one hand.

1932

The first Olympic Village was built for the Los Angeles Games, but only for male athletes. Women stayed in a hotel.

Luol Deng

LUOL was born in Sudan, in Africa, but his family left because of the war there and moved to London when he was 10. He started playing Basketball and represented England at junior level. When he was 14, he moved to America. He was so good at Basketball that he became a professional player with the famous Chicago Bulls team. As a thank-you to the UK for looking after him and his family, he became a British citizen and agreed to captain Britain's Basketball team.

Key Facts

Born: 16 April 1985
Height: 2.0 m
Weight: 100kg
Home town: Wau, Sudan
Event: Basketball

Track Record

2004: Signed professional contract with the Chicago Bulls in the NBA League in America
2004: Picked for NBA all-rookie first team.
2007: NBA Sportsmanship Award
2008: Signed new six-year professional deal with Chicago Bulls worth £40 million

Shoot the hoop

Tick the name of the shot that bounces off the backboard into the basket.

'Basketball has just grown so much with a lot of people talking about it and kids paying attention to it.'

Answer on page 95.

◯ **Bank Shot**

◯ **Bounce Back**

◯ **Big Shot**

1932

Winners were given their medals on a special podium for the first time, while the flag of the champion was raised.

Boxing

Ding ding! Round one here we go!

Boxing is a fighting sport that has been popular since the ancient Olympic Games. It became part of the modern Olympic Games in 1920. The London 2012 Games will be the first to feature women's Boxing. Many Olympic boxers become world famous, just like the great Muhammad Ali.

The lowdown

What? Boxers wear boxing gloves and head guards and score points for punching their opponent. Men box for three periods, or rounds. Each round lasts three minutes. Women box for four rounds of two minutes. Boxers fight against opponents who are around the same weight.
Where? ExCeL London.
Don't miss: Super Heavyweight final.

Believe it or not

Boxing referee Keith Walker was punched by South Korean officials and fans after South Korean boxer Byun Jong-il lost his fight at the 1988 Olympic Games in Seoul. Jong-il was so angry that he refused to leave the ring. He sat on the floor and sulked for 68 minutes!

Jargon buster

THROW IN THE TOWEL: give up before the fight is over. The boxer's helper throws a towel into the ring to tell the referee that the boxer does not want to carry on any more.

Muhammad Ali won gold in the Light Heavyweight category at the Rome 1960 Olympic Games.

Know The Rule

The referee counts to 10 when a boxer is knocked to the floor. If the boxer does not get up by the time the referee has finished counting, the other boxer wins. This is called a 'knock-out'.

1932
US athlete Mildred 'Babe' Didrikson won gold in the 80 metres hurdles and Javelin, plus silver in the High jump!

Khalid Yafai

KHALID is one of the UK's best amateur boxers. Only amateur boxers, who do not get paid, are allowed to compete at the Olympic Games. In 2005 he became the under-17 world champion. A year later he became one of the youngest British champions at the age of 17. He competed at the Olympic Games in Beijing in 2008, but lost to a boxer from Cuba. This has made him determined to win gold in London!

Weigh to go
Match these Olympic boxing weights to their names.

Heavyweight ◯

Welterweight ◯

Flyweight ◯

51 kg	91 kg	69 kg
A	B	C

Answer on page 95.

Key Facts
Born: 11 June 1989
Height: 1.62m
Weight: 51kg
Home town: Moseley
Event: Flyweight

Track Record
2005: Gold medal in the Under-17 World Championships in Liverpool
2006: Gold medal in the Amateur Boxing Association Championships in London
2007: Silver medal in the European Junior Championships in Sombor, Serbia
2008: Competed at the 2008 Olympic Games in Beijing

Khalid Yafai even has a tattoo of the Olympic rings on his arm!

'Everyone wants the medal. Everyone wants to become a hero.'

Cycling

Cycling was Britain's most successful sport at the last Olympic Games. British riders won an amazing eight gold medals in Beijing. There are four different cycling competitions at the Olympic Games: Track Cycling, Road Cycling, BMX and Mountain Bike.

The lowdown

What? Track cyclists race around an oval track in the indoor Velodrome on bikes with just one gear and no brakes! Road cyclists race on the roads, while mountain bikers race over a hilly course. BMX cyclists have a bumpier ride, racing around a short circuit full of jumps and tight corners.
Where? Velodrome, BMX Circuit, Hadleigh Farm in Essex – and the streets of London!
Don't miss: Women's BMX.

Believe it or not

In Antwerp in 1920, the Cycling Road Race contained several railway crossings. Swedish rider Harry Stenqvist thought he had lost the race, but he was later awarded the gold medal when judges discovered that he had been delayed for four minutes by a passing train!

Jargon buster

KEIRIN: a Track Cycling race in which riders follow a small motorbike called a derny. A few laps from the end, the derny leaves the track and the riders power off on a sprint to the finish!

*Former world champion BMX cyclist, **Shanaze Reade**, hopes to be on track for gold!*

Know the rule

BMX riders are not allowed to knock their opponents off their bikes or to block them while they are racing. If they do, judges can disqualify them.

1936

US athlete Jesse Owens won four gold medals: 100 metres, 200m, 4 x 100m relay and the Long jump!

Victoria Pendleton

VICTORIA was born into a bike-mad family and began cycling almost as soon as she could walk. She used to race against her twin brother on a grass track. Later she started to train hard and became part of the British team. Victoria competed at the Olympic Games in Athens in 2004, but sadly failed to win a medal. She tried again at the Olympics in Beijing in 2008 and this time she won the gold medal!

Cycling is a wheely cool sport!

Whizzing wheels
What time did Victoria achieve to take the Olympic record for the 200m sprint?

1 hour, 963 seconds ◯

100.963 seconds ◯

10.963 seconds ◯

Answer on page 95.

Victoria Pendleton on her track bike at the Beijing Games.

Key Facts
Born: 24 September 1980
Height: 1.65m
Weight: 62kg
Home town: Hitchin
Event: Track sprint, Team sprint and Keirin

Track Record
2005–2010: Eight gold medals at World Championships for Sprint and Team sprint events
2008: Gold medal in Sprint at the Olympic Games in Beijing

'I hope to inspire a new generation of girls and boys on bikes.'

Equestrian

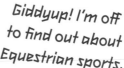

Equestrian is the name given to Olympic sports that involve horses. There are three main competitions: Jumping, Dressage and Eventing. Equestrian is the only Olympic sport where women and men compete against each other.

Giddyup! I'm off to find out about Equestrian sports.

Oliver Townend riding Flint Curtis in the jumping part of the Eventing competition.

The lowdown

What? In Jumping, riders and horses are timed as they jump a series of fences. They lose points if they knock any fences down. In Dressage, riders and horses perform a series of movements that are awarded points by judges. Eventing combines jumping, dressage and cross-country riding into one all-round event.
Where? Greenwich Park.
Don't miss: Women's Eventing.

Believe it or not

Until 1952 only male military officers were allowed to compete in Dressage. In 1948 the Swedish team was disqualified and lost its gold medal when it was discovered that team member Gehnäll Persson was not an officer!

Jargon buster

FAULT: a set number of penalty points that are given to Jumping competitors if they make a mistake like knocking down a fence.

Know the rule

Dressage competitors can be disqualified if they are not wearing the correct clothing. Riders must even use the correct saddle, spurs and helmet!

1936
The Olympic Flame was lit at the site of the ancient Games in Olympia and carried to Berlin in the first Olympic Torch Relay.

Zara Phillips

ZARA PHILLIPS is the Queen's granddaughter. Her mother is Anne, Princess Royal, who competed for Britain in Eventing at the 1976 Olympic Games in Montreal. Zara also takes part in Eventing and won the World Championship in 2006. She is hoping to compete in her first Olympic Games in London. She was all set to take part in the Games in Beijing in 2008, but she had to stay at home because her horse, Toytown, was injured.

'It's a great sport, even if there are dangers. I love the risk of it.'

Zara Phillips riding *Glenbuck in a Jumping event.*

Saddle up!
What is the highest fence in an Olympic Jumping event?

Answer on page 95.

○ **1 metre**

○ **1.6 metres**

○ **10 metres**

Key Facts
Born: 15 May 1981
Height: 1.68m
Weight: 64kg
Home town: Cheltenham
Event: Eventing

london 2012

Track Record
2005: Gold medal in team and individual competitions at the European Eventing Championships in Blenheim

2006: Individual gold medal and team silver medal at the World Eventing Championships in Aachen

Football

My goal is to find out about Football!

Football is the most popular team sport in the world. Men's Football has been played at the Olympic Games since 1908, when Britain won the first ever Football gold medal. Women's Football joined the Olympic Games in 1996.

The lowdown

What? Football is a ball game for teams of 11 players. Footballers use their feet, heads or bodies to score goals by putting the ball in the other team's net. Only goalkeepers are allowed to touch the ball with their hands.

Where? Wembley Stadium, Old Trafford, Millennium Stadium, St James' Park, City of Coventry Stadium and Hampden Park.

Don't miss: The finals at Wembley.

Believe it or not

When Cameroon won the Football gold medal at the Sydney 2000 Olympics, the president of Cameroon was so excited he gave everyone in his country a day off work to celebrate!

Jargon buster

EXTRA-TIME: at the Olympic Games, if a Football match is still level after 90 minutes in the knockout rounds, the teams play an extra 30 minutes to decide the winner. If the score is still level after extra time, the match is decided by a penalty shoot-out.

Know the rule

Men's Olympic Football is for players under the age of 23, but teams are allowed to pick up to three older players. In the women's competition, players can be any age.

Professional players have been allowed to play in the Games since 1992, so you can watch world famous players in action!

1948

London hosted the Games for the second time. Money was tight after the Second World War, so Holland helped by donating 100 tons of fruit!

Kelly Smith

KELLY used to play in boys' football teams when she was growing up. Now she is one of the best and most famous female footballers in the world. She is a striker who scored lots of goals for Arsenal Ladies before moving to America in 2009 to join Boston Breakers. She made her first appearance for England when she was only 16 and has been playing for her country ever since.

Key Facts
Born: 29 October 1978
Height: 1.68m
Weight: 62kg
Home town: Watford
Event: Football

Track Record
2001–2009: Competed in three European Championships and one World Cup. Runner-up with England at Euro 2009 in Finland
2006, 2008, 2009: Reached final shortlist for the Women's World Player of the Year award

london

Golden goals
Which country has won a record-breaking three gold medals for Football?

Argentina

Brazil

Hungary

Kelly Smith is one of the world's best women footballers.

Answer on page 95.

'It would be amazing to say one had played in a World Cup and an Olympics.'

1948
Sir Ludwig Guttmann organised sports competitions for injured soldiers. This was the start of the Paralympic Games.

Gymnastics

Gymnasts amaze audiences with their agility, strength and skill. There are three types of event at the Olympic Games: Artistic, Rhythmic and Trampoline. Artistic Gymnastics is the best-known and attracts huge crowds.

Gee up! Whoops. Wrong type of horse!

The lowdown

What? In Artistic Gymnastics, athletes perform using apparatus. Men compete in six events: Floor, Pommel horse, Rings, Vault, Parallel bars and Horizontal bar. Women have four events: Vault, Uneven bars, Balance beam and Floor. Rhythmic gymnasts perform to music and use ropes, hoops, balls, clubs or ribbons. In Trampoline, gymnasts can bounce 10 metres!
Where? North Greenwich Arena, Wembley Arena.
Don't miss: Women's All-around final.

Believe it or not

Dimitrios Loundras, a Greek gymnast, competed at the 1896 Olympic Games when he was only 10 years old. He won a bronze medal in the Team parallel bars event, but there were only three teams taking part. He is the youngest athlete ever to take part in the Olympics.

Jargon buster

ALL-AROUND: a type of Artistic gymnast who competes in every event in the hope of becoming the overall, or All-around champion. Some gymnasts compete on just one or two pieces of apparatus.

Know the rule

Gymnasts have to be at least 16 years old to take part in the Olympic Games these days.

Beth Tweddle is the UK's most successful gymnast, and has a good chance of winning Olympic gold!

1952

Czech soldier Emil Zatopek made history at the Helsinki Games by winning gold in the 5,000 metres, 10,000m and the Marathon!

Daniel Keatings

DANIEL joined a gymnastics club when he was five years old. He entered his first national championship when he was nine and won the gold medal. At 10 he was selected for the British team. He has won many medals in junior and senior competitions. His biggest achievement was in 2009 in London when he became the first British gymnast to win an All-around medal at a World Championships. He finished second, but aims to win the gold medal at the Olympic Games in London!

*Gymnasts like **Daniel Keatings** need a mix of muscle and skill to master the pommel horse.*

Horse play?
A pommel horse was first used by soldiers to practise getting on a real horse?

True ⃝　False ⃝

Answer on page 95.

'The World Championships have given me a taste of what London will be like in 2012.'

Key Facts
Born: 28 January 1986
Height: 1.65m
Weight: 57kg
Home town: Sheffield
Event: All-around

Track Record
2007: Silver medal in Pommel horse at the European Championships in Amsterdam

2008: Four gold medals at the European Junior Championships in Lausanne

2009: Silver medal (All-around) and bronze medal (Pommel horse) at the European Championships in Milan

2009: Silver medal in All-around at the World Championships in London

1952
The Soviet Union took part in the Games for the first time. Nina Romashkova won the country's first ever gold medal in the Discus.

Rowing

Whizzing along on the water is great fun!

Britain has won a Rowing gold medal at every Olympic Games since 1984. Rowing was set to be part of the first modern Olympics in Athens in 1896, but it was cancelled because the sea was too rough!

The lowdown

What? All Rowing races are held over 2,000 metres. Rowers can race as individuals, in pairs or in teams of four or eight. In sculling races, rowers have two oars. In sweep boat races, each rower has one oar. Boats with eight rowers are steered by an extra person called the coxswain, or 'cox'.

Where? Eton Dorney.

Don't miss: Men's and women's eights finals.

Jargon buster

CATCHING A CRAB: when rowers make a mistake by getting their oar stuck in the water, slowing their boat down.

Believe it or not

At the 1928 Olympic Games in Amsterdam, Australian Bobby Pearce stopped halfway through his quarter-final sculling race to let a family of ducks pass in front of his boat. He still won the race!

Know the rule

Three of the 14 Olympic Rowing races are for lightweight Rowers. Rowers in the men's lightweight race must be under 72.5kg and female lightweights under 59kg.

Rowers race with their backs to the finish line. It is the only 'backwards' sport in the Games!

1952

The rules changed so that women were allowed to compete against men in Equestrian events for the first time.

Zac Purchase

ZAC started rowing at school when he was 13 and was soon winning medals. He was so good that he didn't lose a race for six years! At 20 he became a world champion in a single sculling boat or scull. In 2008 he teamed up with Mark Hunter to row in a two-person scull. They didn't lose a race all year and won gold at the Beijing 2008 Olympic Games. Zac was so overjoyed, that he cried at the medal ceremony.

Key Facts
Born: 5 May 1986
Height: 1.84m
Weight: 73kg
Home town: Cheltenham
Event: Lightweight double sculls

Track Record
2005: Silver medal in Lightweight single scull at the World Championships
2006: Gold medal in Lightweight single scull at the World Championships
2008: Gold medal in Lightweight double sculls at the Beijing 2008 Games

Answer on page 95.

Name game
What is another name that rowers use for a racing boat?

○ **Raft**

○ **Log**

○ **Shell**

*Zac Purchase (right) and team-mate **Mark Hunter** after winning the Men's lightweight double sculls at the Beijing 2008 Games.*

GREAT BRITAIN

'London will be an astonishing Games to be part of, let alone to be winning.'

Sailing

Sailing is one of the UK's top Olympic sports. British sailors won four gold medals at the Beijing 2008 Games. Sailing has been part of the Olympic Games since 1908. In 2012, all the Sailing events will take place on the sea at Weymouth and Portland.

The lowdown

What? There are 10 Olympic events for different types of boat or windsurfing board. Boats vary in size and weight and can hold one, two or three sailors. Men and women compete separately in a series of races on the sea.

Where? Weymouth Bay and Portland Harbour.

Don't miss: Men's Finn medal race.

Believe it or not

At the 1968 Olympic Games in Mexico, Canadian sailor Lawrence Lemieux stopped to rescue a competitor whose boat had sunk. Lemieux finished 21, but was given a special Olympic medal for his kindness.

Jargon buster

REGATTA: the name given to a whole series of Sailing races.

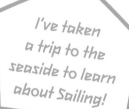

I've taken a trip to the seaside to learn about Sailing!

GBR

Know the rule

Sailors earn points for where they finish in each race. The winner gets one point, second gets two points, third place three, and so on. The gold medal goes to the sailor or sailors with the lowest overall score at the end.

1956

Melbourne hosted the Games, but strict rules about bringing animals into Australia meant that Equestrian events were held in Sweden!

Ben Ainslie

'My greatest strength is that I never give up.'

BEN is the most successful Olympic sailor Britain has ever seen. He grew up near the sea in Cornwall and started sailing when he was eight. By the age of 16 he was already a world champion. At 19 he won a silver medal at his first Olympic Games in Athens, sailing solo in a Laser class dinghy. Since then he has won three gold medals at three different Olympic Games. He will be trying to win his fourth gold medal at the London 2012 Games.

Ben holds up his gold medal for single-handedly sailing a Finn class dinghy to victory at the Beijing 2008 Games.

Nautical know-how
Tick the Olympic Sailing boat that is sailed by a crew of two!

Answer on page 95.

○ **Laser**

○ **Finn**

○ **49er**

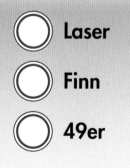

Key Facts

Born: 5 February 1977
Height: 1.82m
Weight: 80kg
Home town: Restronguet
Event: Sailing, Finn class

Track Record
1996: Silver medal in Laser class at the Olympic Games in Atlanta
2000: Gold medal in Laser class at the Olympic Games in Sydney
2004: Gold medal in Finn class at the Olympic Games in Athens
2008: Gold medal in Finn class at the Olympic Games in Beijing

1956
Melbourrne held the first Closing Ceremony where athletes entered the stadium together rather than in their separate national teams.

Paralympic sports

More than 4,000 athletes will compete in the London 2012 Paralympic Games. Here's the essential info on the 20 different Paralympic sports!

 Archery

Athletes shoot arrows at targets 70 metres away in both standing and wheelchair competitions.

 Athletics

There are Track races over a range of distances, plus Field events involving throwing and jumping.

 Boccia

A game of accuracy as competitors throw a ball to land the closest to a target ball, or 'jack'.

 Cycling – Road

Riders race on roads using bicycles, tricycles, tandems or hand cycles. There are both team and individual events.

 Cycling – Track

Cyclists race in the Velodrome on various bikes, including tandems for visually impaired athletes.

 Equestrian

A Dressage competition in which riders and their horses are marked for their performance.

 Football 5-a-side

A game for visually-impaired athletes using a ball with a bell inside it.

 Football 7-a-side

Footballers with cerebral palsy compete in teams of seven. Matches last for 60 minutes.

 Goalball

Visually impaired athletes try to roll a ball which has a bell inside it into their opponents' net.

Just look at all these sports! Which one shall I try first?

1960

The Olympic Games in Rome were broadcast live on TV to 18 European countries, plus the USA, Canada and Japan.

Judo

A martial art for visually impaired athletes that involves throws and holds.

Powerlifting

Athletes lie on their backs and push a bar with weights on it above their chests.

Rowing

Races are held over 1,000 metres for both individual rowers and crews of two and four.

Sailing

Sailors score points over eleven individual yacht races to find the overall winner.

Shooting

Competitors shoot rifles or pistols at a fixed target from 10, 25 or 50 metres away.

Swimming

Athletes race in a 50-metre pool against other competitors of similar physical ability.

Table Tennis

Players sit on the floor and hit a ball over a net with a bat to score points.

Volleyball – Sitting

Players sitting on the floor pass a ball back and forth over a net to score points.

Wheelchair Basketball

Teams of five players in wheelchairs try to throw a ball through their opponents' basket.

Wheelchair Fencing

Modern-day sword fighting for athletes in wheelchairs that are fastened to the floor.

Wheelchair Rugby

Teams of four wheelchair athletes try to carry a ball across their opponents' goal-line.

Wheelchair Tennis

The game follows the same rules as Tennis, but the ball is allowed to bounce twice.

1960
The first official Paralympic Games were held in Rome, starting six days after the Closing Ceremony of the Olympic Games.

Paralympic gold!

UK Paralympic athletes are among the best in the world. They won an amazing 42 gold medals at the last Paralympic Games. Let's cheer them on to win even more in London!

The United Kingdom has a proud tradition in the Paralympic Games. The first ever sporting competitions between athletes with a disability took place in Britain in 1948. This led to the Paralympic Games as we know them today. Nowadays, thousands of athletes take part in 20 different sports. The UK team is always one of the strongest. In Beijing in 2008, the team won a total of 102 medals!

More than 300 UK athletes are expected to take part in the 2012 Paralympic Games in London. This increase on the 212 athletes at the last Paralympic Games in Beijing will make it the biggest UK team in Paralympic history.

Wheelchair racer Baroness Tanni Grey-Thompson and swimmer David Roberts are the most successful UK athletes in Paralympic history. They have identical Paralympic records of 11 gold medals, four silver medals and one bronze medal. Tanni was made a baroness and has now retired from competing at the Paralympic Games, but David is still competing and he hopes to win even more Paralympic medals in London.

Britain has finished second in the medals table at the last three Paralympic Games in 2000, 2004 and 2008. The most medals that Britain has ever won at a Paralympic Games is 183. That was in Seoul in 1988.

Swimmer Chris Holmes holds the record for winning the most gold medals at a single Paralympic Games. He won six of them in Barcelona in 1992.

In 2012, the Paralympic Games will be hosted in London for the very first time!

1964
The Tokyo Olympic Games were the first to be held in Asia and featured two new sports: Judo and Volleyball.

Paralympic stars

Swimmer Joanne Round was just 12 years old when she won a relay gold medal at the 1988 Paralympic Games in Seoul. She is Britain's youngest Paralympic champion. Eleanor Simmonds is the youngest athlete to win a gold medal in an individual race. She was 13 when she won two Swimming gold medals in Beijing in 2008. Eleanor will be one of the stars of the British team at the London 2012 Games.

Pedals and medals

Britain's best sport at the last Paralympic Games in Beijing was Cycling. The British riders won 17 gold medals and three silver medals. They also set lots of world records along the way.

London 2012 will be the 14th official Paralympic Games. The cities that hosted the previous 13 are below.

Paralympic Games

1960 .....Rome
1964 .....Tokyo
1968 .....Tel Aviv
1972 .....Heidelberg
1976 .....Toronto
1980 .....Arnhem
1984 .....Stoke Mandeville & New York
1988 .....Seoul
1992 .....Barcelona
1996 .....Atlanta
2000 .....Sydney
2004 .....Athens
2008 .....Beijing

The Paralympic Games are going to be awesome!

1964
Wheelchair racing was added to the Paralympic Games in Tokyo to make nine Paralympic sports events in total.

Paralympic Athletics

Athletics is the biggest Paralympic sport. On the track, wheelchair races, with their high-speed thrills and spills, always draw the crowds. There are also field events for athletes who throw and jump.

Ready, steady... go!

The lowdown

What? Paralympic athletes compete against other athletes with a similar disability. Track races are held over the same distances as Olympic track races, from 100 metres to the Marathon. There are seven field events: Shot put, Discus, Javelin, Club-throwing, Long jump, High jump and Triple jump.
Where? Olympic Stadium and out on the streets of London.
Don't miss: Marathon.

Believe it or not

American runner Marla Runyan, who is visually impaired, has competed at both the Olympic Games and Paralympic Games. She won five Paralympic gold medals and then qualified for the Sydney 2000 Olympic Games, where she finished eighth in the final of the 1,500 metres.

Jargon buster

CLASSIFICATION: to make things fair, every Paralympic athlete is given a special code to make sure they compete against athletes with a similar disability.

Know the rule

Wheelchair athletes are not allowed to block opponents who are trying to go past them during a race.

Shelly Woods powers down the track. Shelly is one of the UKs top wheelchair racers.

1968

In Mexico, American long jumper Bob Beamon leapt an incredible 8.90 metres. It remained a world record for 22 years!

David Weir

DAVID is Britain's fastest wheelchair racer. He took part in his first Paralympic Games in Atlanta in 1996 when he was just 17 years old. He has won six Paralympic medals, including two gold medals. He is the fastest British racer in history at every distance up to 5,000 metres. He is also the fastest in long-distance road races such as the Half-marathon and Marathon. He hopes to be the best again at the Paralympic Games in his home city of London.

Marathon measure?
What distance is a Paralympic Marathon race held over?

○ 4.195 kilometres

○ 42.195 kilometres

○ 24.195 kilometres

Answer on page 95.

Key Facts
Born: 5 June 1979
Home town: Sutton, Surrey
Event: Wheelchair racing
(T54 disability class)

Paralympic Games

Track Record
2004: Silver medal in 100 metres and bronze medal in 200 metres at the Paralympic Games in Athens
2008: Gold medals in 800 metres and 1,500m metres, a silver medal in 400 metres and a bronze medal in 5,000 metres at the Paralympic Games in Beijing

*Elite wheelchair athlete **David Weir** won two gold medals at the 2008 Paralympic Games and holds a stack of British track records.*

'Every race I enter, I aim to win.'

1968
The Paralympic Games were held in Israel, where Italy's Roberto Marson won an astounding nine gold medals!

Paralympic Cycling

Paralympic Cycling is speedy and exciting to watch! The UK's Cycling team is the best in the world and won an incredible 17 gold medals at the Beijing Paralympic Games. As well as races for pedal bikes, there are also hand cycle races.

Pedal power is the wheel deal in this sport!

Juan Jose Mendez in the Men's 1 kilometre time trial at the 2008 Beijing Paralympic Games.

The lowdown

What? Paralympic Cycling has the same rules as the Olympic sport, but there are four types of bicycle: bikes with two wheels, tricycles with three wheels, hand cycles that cyclists pedal with their arms and bicycles for two people. Riders race against riders with the same kind of disability.

Where? Velodrome and central London.

Don't miss: Men's team sprint.

Jargon buster

TANDEM: a bike for two people. Tandems are used by Paralympic athletes who are blind or who have difficulty seeing. The athlete sits on the back saddle while a guide who can see sits on the front saddle.

Know the rule

Paralympic tandem guides do not have to be disabled, but they can't be professional cyclists. Cyclists who have recently competed for their country are also not allowed to be guides.

Believe it or not

Spanish cyclist Juan Jose Mendez does not have a left leg or a left arm, but he still won a bronze medal at the Paralympic Games in 2008.

1972
American swimmer Mark Spitz was the star of the Munich Olympic Games, winning seven gold medals in the pool.

Darren Kenny

DARREN started racing bikes when he was 11 years old, but at the age of 18 he had a very bad bike crash during a race called the Junior Tour of Ireland, injuring his head and neck. He now competes as a Paralympic track cyclist and is one of the best in the world. He won four gold medals at the 2008 Paralympic Games in Beijing. He hopes to win five at the 2012 Games in London!

Key Facts
Born: 17 March 1970
Home town: Verwood
Event: Cycling
(CP3 disability class)

Track Record
2004: Two gold medals and one silver at the Paralympic Games in Athens
2005–2008: Nine gold medals, three silver medals and two bronze medals at various World Disability Championships
2008: Four gold medals and one silver at the Paralympic Games in Beijing

On Track for gold
In which year was Track Cycling introduced as a Paralympic event?

◯ **1988 Seoul**

◯ **2008 Beijing**

◯ **1996 Atlanta**

Answer on page 95.

'Hard work is the key to success, whatever situation you are in.'

Darren Kenny has won Paralympic gold for Cycling both on the road and on the track.

1972
The Heidelberg Paralympic Games saw America beat Israel by just one point in the Wheelchair basketball final!

Paralympic Swimming

Swimming has been a Paralympic sport since the first Paralympic Games in Rome in 1960. Swimmers from more than 80 countries take part, making it one of the largest sports. British Paralympic swimmers won 10 gold medals at the last Games in Beijing.

The lowdown

What? Paralympic swimmers race each other over distances from 50 metres to 400 metres. There are races for all four strokes: freestyle (crawl), breaststroke, backstroke and butterfly. Swimmers compete against other swimmers with a similar physical ability.
Where? Aquatics Centre.
Don't miss: Women's 400m freestyle (S6)

Believe it or not

South African swimmer Natalie du Toit, who has one leg, competed at the Olympic Games as well as the Paralympics in Beijing in 2008. She finished 16th in the 10 kilometre race at the Olympic Games and then won five gold medals at the Paralympic Games.

Jargon buster

TAPPER: a person who helps blind swimmers know when they are getting close to the end of the swimming pool by tapping them gently on the head with a long rod with a soft tip. When swimmers feel the tap, they know they have to get ready to turn!

I want to make a splash at the Paralympic Games!

*Swimmer **Natalie du Toit** is one of five athletes who have competed at both the Olympic Games and the Paralympic Games.*

1976
Romanian gymnast Nadia Comaneci became the first to score 10 out of 10 on the uneven bars at the Montreal Games!

Eleanor Simmonds

ELEANOR, or 'Ellie' as she is known, was just 13 when she won two gold medals at the 2008 Paralympic Games in Beijing. She is the youngest British athlete ever to win a Paralympic gold medal. She was born with a disability called dwarfism, but learned to swim when she was only four. She took part in her first race when she was eight. After her amazing achievement in Beijing, she became the youngest person to receive a special award from the Queen called an MBE.

Key Facts
Born: 11 November 1994
Home town: Walsall
Event: Swimming, freestyle and butterfly (S6 disability class)

Track Record
2008: Gold medals for 100 metres and 400m freestyle at the Beijing Paralympic Games
2010: World records in 100 metres and 400m freestyle and 200m individual medley at the World Championships in Holland

Gold mine
How many gold medals has Paralympic swimmer David Roberts won?

8   11   5

Answer on page 95.

Ellie Simmonds with her two Paralympic gold medals from the Beijing Games.

'I can't believe I'm a Paralympic champion.'

1976
In Toronto, amputees and visually impaired athletes competed for the first time at the Paralympic Games.

Wheelchair Basketball

The fast-moving action of Wheelchair Basketball makes it a firm favourite with fans. It was invented in America as a sport for soldiers injured in the Second World War. It first became a part of the Paralympic Games in 1960.

The lowdown

What? Wheelchair Basketball has similar rules to running basketball. The court is the same size and the baskets the same height. Each team has five players who try to get the ball into the other team's basket. Players must move the ball by passing or bouncing.
Where? Basketball Arena and North Greenwich Arena.
Don't miss: The thrilling finals!

You've got to move fast to score in this sport!

Believe it or not

The world's best players use special wheelchairs made out of a metal called titanium. Each wheelchair can cost more than £3,500, but might last just six months before the player wears it out and needs a new one!

Jargon buster

TRAVELLING: when players touch the wheels of their wheelchair more than twice without bouncing the ball, passing, or shooting. This is against the rules, so if a player is caught travelling the ball is given to the other team.

Know the rule

If a player falls out of a wheelchair during a match and there is a danger of the player being injured, the game is stopped straight away.

Ade Adepitan is one of Britain's best-known players and a Paralympic bronze medal winner.

1980
At the Moscow Games, Soviet gymnast Alexander Dityatin won a medal in all eight events, including three gold medals.

Jon Pollock

JON was born with spina bifida and started playing Wheelchair Basketball when he was 15. Now he is one of the best players in the world. He was captain of the British team at the last Paralympic Games in Beijing. At the Games, Britain won the bronze medal thanks to Jon. He scored 31 points in the deciding match against Holland. He would dearly love to win another Paralympic medal in London.

Key Facts

Born: 11 May 1977
Home town: Wigan
Event: Wheelchair Basketball

London 2012
Paralympic Games

Track Record
2004: Bronze medal for Britain in Wheelchair Basketball at the Paralympic Games in Athens
2008: Bronze medal for Britain in Wheelchair Basketball at the Paralympic Games in Beijing

Evenly matched
If the teams are level in Wheelchair Basketball they must play on until one side wins?

True   False

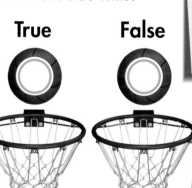

Answer on page 95.

'We are competing with the elite of the world right now.'

To be a top player like **Jon Pollock** you need a mix of strength and skill.

1980
Canada's Arnie Boldt won the High jump at the Paralympic Games by leaping an amazing 1.96 metres!

Split-second timing

A fraction of a second can make the difference between winning a gold or a silver medal, so it's very important to have accurate timing at the Games. In the early days, a hand-held stopwatch was used, but today athletes are timed with the latest electronic gadgets.

It's a race against the clock!

At the last Olympic Games in Beijing, the American swimmer Michael Phelps won the seventh of his eight gold medals in the 100 metres butterfly. But most people watching thought he had been beaten by Serbian swimmer Milorad Cavic. Then the electronic timer revealed that Phelps had finished in 50.58 seconds and that Cavic was just one hundredth of a second slower. The clock had stopped the moment Phelps touched an electronic contact pad. He had won by a finger tip.

Everyone's eyes are on the scoreboard after an event to see those all-important results!

Believe it or not

The final of the Women's 100 metres in Atlanta in 1996 was one of the closest races in history. A photo finish showed that American athlete Gail Devers had beaten the Jamaican runner Merlene Ottey by five thousandths of a second. She was just two centimetres ahead at the finish line.

1984
Following a glittering Hollywood-style Opening Ceremony, 140 nations took part in the Los Angeles Olympic Games.

Off like a shot

The bang of the starting pistol is the signal for track athletes to start running! The pistol also starts the automatic timing equipment. As the runners cross the finish line, a camera takes photographs of them up to 3,000 times each second. This 'photo finish' means that the race times of the runners are accurate to within one three-thousandth of a second – that's more than 300 times quicker than it takes to blink!

High-tech starting pistols make a bang and start the clock in exactly the same instant.

Just for the record

When track and field athletes compete, their times and distances are displayed on an electronic scoreboard in the stadium. If the scoreboard also shows the letters 'WR', it means that an athlete has broken the world record – it's the best performance in history! The letters 'PB' mean 'personal best', which means it is the best time or distance that the athlete has ever achieved.

The finishing touch

In track races, athletes automatically stop the clock the moment their torso, or chest, touches the finish line. That is why athletes always dip forward at the end of a race, pushing their chests out towards the line.

Usain Bolt *wins in a photo finish of the Men's 100 metres at Beijing 2008.*

1984
Sebastian Coe won another gold medal in the 1,500 metres and Daley Thompson won his second gold in the Decathlon.

Faster!

> If you want to be first, you have to be fast!

The Olympic motto, 'Faster, Higher, Stronger', is about always trying to do better. To win gold in many Olympic and Paralympic sports that means you have to go faster!

Lightning speed

45km/h

Jamaican athlete Usain Bolt is the fastest sprinter on the planet. He holds world records of 9.58 seconds for the 100 metres and 19.19 seconds for the 200 metres. No wonder he is known as 'Lightning Bolt'.

Bolt's top running speed is an astonishing 45 kilometres per hour, which is almost as fast as a galloping horse!

Marathon man

20.3km/h

Ethiopian Haile Gebrselassie is considered the greatest long-distance runner of all time. He holds the world record for the Marathon, which is 42.195 kilometres long. His time is 2 hours, 3 minutes, 59 seconds.

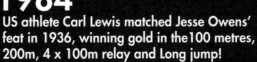

1984
US athlete Carl Lewis matched Jesse Owens' feat in 1936, winning gold in the 100 metres, 200m, 4 x 100m relay and Long jump!

Wheely fast

Heinz Frei, of Switzerland, is the world record-holder for the Wheelchair Marathon with a time of 1 hour, 20 minutes, 14 seconds. The quickest woman is Italian Francesca Porcelleto with a time of 1 hour, 38 minutes, 29 seconds.

31.5km/h

Rapid riders

Britain's four-man cycling team broke the world record in the 4 kilometre pursuit at the Beijing 2008 Games, setting a time of 3 minutes, 53.314 seconds. They were travelling at over 69km/h – that's enough for a speeding ticket in some areas!

69.2km/h

Super-fast swimmer

The fastest swimming race is the men's 50 metres freestyle. Brazilian Cesar Cielo holds the world record of 20.91 seconds. The race is over so quickly that many swimmers hold their breath from start to finish.

8.6km/h

1984

The Paralympic Games were split between Stoke Mandeville, UK and New York. The first Marathon for wheelchair athletes was held.

Higher!

High jumpers and pole vaulters jump up. Divers travel down. Trampolinists do both! But they all need the maximum height to win a gold medal!

High jumpers!

Javier Sotomayor

Cuban high jumper Javier Sotomayor cleared an incredible 2.45 metres in 1993. That is higher than the ceiling in most houses! It is the highest jump ever achieved by a human being.

I'm going to see how high I can bounce!

2.45m

With 17 of the 24 all-time best jumps to his credit, **Javier** is the greatest high jumper ever.

2.09m

Stefka Kostadinova

Bulgarian athlete Stefka Kostadinova set a Women's High jump world record of 2.09 metres in 1987. The High jump bar was higher than a door in most homes. It was even higher than Luol Deng, Britain's Basketball captain!

1988
In Seoul, the Paralympic Games were held in the same venues as the Olympic Games for the first time.

Pole position!

Sergey Bubka

Sergey Bubka, a pole vaulter from Ukraine, broke 35 world records during his career. His vault of 6.14 metres in 1994 is still the highest in history. It was even higher than a fully grown giraffe!

6.14m

Sky dive

10m

Tom Daley

In Diving, the highest dive is from a 10-metre platform – that's higher than a two-storey house! Divers, such as the UK's Tom Daley, leap up to gain extra time in the air. They have less than two seconds before they hit the water.

High flyer

Yelena Isinbayeva

Russia's Yelena Isinbayeva, the world's greatest female pole vaulter, became the first woman to clear a height of five metres in 2005. That is higher than a double-decker London bus.

5m

1988

Trischa Zorn, a visually-impaired American swimmer, won 12 gold medals and set nine world records at the Paralympic Games!

Stronger!

You need massive muscles to win a Weightlifting medal!

Some Olympic and Paralympic events call for amazing feats of strength. The strongest athletes can be found in the Weightlifting and throwing competitions.

Weightlifting wonders

Hossein Rezazadeh

In 2004, Iranian weightlifter Hossein Rezazadeh lifted a world record 263.5 kilograms. That is the same as lifting four average-sized people above his head. It is the heaviest weight ever lifted by a human being in a weightlifting competition.

263.5kg

Jang Mi-Ran

The heaviest weight ever lifted by a woman is 186 kilograms – that's about the same as lifting two full-grown men! It was achieved by South Korea's Jang Mi-Ran at the 2008 Beijing Olympic Games.

186kg

1988

At the Seoul Games in South Korea, Tennis returned as an Olympic sport after a gap of 64 years.

Super shot

In the Shot put, athletes hurl a heavy metal 'shot', or ball, as far as possible. The men's shot weighs 7.26 kilograms, which is the same as 18 large cans of baked beans. The world record-holder is American Randy Barnes. In 1990 he threw a shot 23.12 metres – nearly twice the length of a bus.

Kazem Rajabi Golojeh

Paralympic weightlifters are called powerlifters. They lie on their backs and push a bar of weights up until their arms are locked. The heaviest weight ever lifted by a Paralympian is a massive 265kg by Iran's Kazem Rajabi Golojeh.

265kg

Zoe Smith

Could you lift the equivalent of a heavy man above your head? Zoe Smith did just that at the age of 14, when she lifted 95 kilograms! Zoe is the UK's most promising female weightlifter and hopes to compete at the 2012 Games.

95kg

1988

Table Tennis made its first appearance at the Seoul Games, with South Korea and China topping the medal tables.

Going for gold

A gold medal is the ultimate prize for Olympic and Paralympic athletes. Winners are presented with their medals on a special podium. It is a great honour and a fitting reward for years of hard work and training.

> It must feel awesome to win a gold medal!

Solid gold

Gold medals were made out of solid gold at the Olympic Games in 1904, 1908 and 1912. Today, they are made mainly from silver, but they must still contain at least six grams of real gold. There are also silver medals for athletes finishing second and bronze medals for those finishing in third place.

A shiny gold medal! There is a brand new medal design for each Olympic Games.

Belive it or not

During the first modern Games, held in Athens in 1896, winners were given a silver medal and an olive branch instead of a gold medal. Runners-up received a bronze medal and a laurel branch.

*Cyclist **Sir Chris Hoy** became the first UK athlete to win three gold medals at the 2008 Beijing Games.*

1992
Part of the city of Barcelona in Spain was completely rebuilt to host the Games, which attracted a record 169 nations!

Record breakers

American swimmer Michael Phelps set a record by winning eight Olympic gold medals at the Beijing 2008 Games. He also won six gold medals at the Olympic Games in Athens in 2004. That makes him the most successful Olympic athlete in history. The most successful Paralympic athlete of all time is also American. Visually impaired swimmer Trischa Zorn won an incredible 41 Paralympic gold medals between 1980 and 1996.

Paralympic swimmer **Trischa Zorn** *races for the finish.*

Medal Match Up!

For which sport did each of these countries top the medal table at the last Olympic Games? Match the sports to the flags.

USA
31 medals
    Boxing

GB
14 medals
    Judo

China
18 medals
    Gymnastics

Cuba
8 medals
    Cycling

Japan
7 medals
    Swimming

Answers on page 95.

Final Olympic medals table: Beijing 2008

Country	Gold	Silver	Bronze	Total
China	51	21	28	100
USA	36	38	36	110
Russia	23	21	28	72
CB	19	13	15	47
Germany	16	10	15	41

1992
Professional Basketball players were allowed to compete for the first time. The American team included Michael Jordan and won the gold!

Olympic legends

There have been many amazing performances by Olympic athletes over the years. Some have even won gold medals in more than one Games. Here are some of the greatest Olympic athletes ever!

Who is your all-time Olympic favourite?

Jim Thorpe (USA)

Jim is considered to be one of the greatest all-round Olympic athletes in history. In 1912, he became the only athlete ever to win gold medals in both the Decathlon and the Modern pentathlon at the same Games.

Jesse Owens (USA)

The son of a poor farmer was the most outstanding athlete of the 1936 Olympic Games in Berlin. Jesse won four gold medals in the 100 metres, 200m, 4 x100m relay and the Long jump!

1992
The Barcelona Paralympic Games were a great success. The Opening Ceremony drew a massive crowd of 65,000 fans.

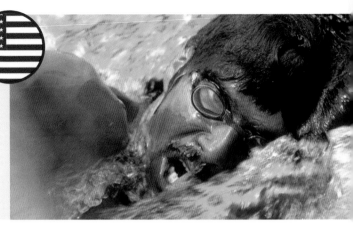

Mark Spitz (USA)

After winning two Swimming gold medals in 1968, he won an incredible seven gold medals for Swimming at the Munich Games in 1972. His achievement remained a record until it was beaten by Michael Phelps in 2008.

Olga Korbut (Soviet Union)

Olga Korbut became a worldwide star at the age of 17 with her brilliant Gymnastics performances in 1972. She won three gold medals and one silver medal, and went on to win another gold and silver in 1976.

Nadia Comaneci (Romania)

In 1976 Nadia became the first gymnast ever to achieve a perfect score of 10 for her performance on the uneven bars. She was just 14. Over the 1976 and 1980 Games she won a total of five gold medals, three silvers and a bronze.

1992

In total, 1.5 million spectators enjoyed the action at the Paralympic Games in Barcelona. Millions more tuned in on TV!

Vasily Alekseyev (Soviet Union)

Vasily, once known as the world's strongest man, is still considered the greatest super heavyweight weightlifter of all-time. He won Olympic gold in 1972 and 1976 and set 80 world records!

Teófilo Stevenson (Cuba)

Teófilo won heavyweight Boxing gold medals in 1972, 1976 and 1980 and is one of only three boxers to win three Olympic gold medals. He might well have won a fourth in Los Angeles in 1984, but Cuba did not take part in those Games.

Steve Redgrave celebrates victory in the Coxless Fours and his fifth gold medal at the Sydney 2000 Games.

Sir Steve Redgrave (GB)

He is Britain's most successful Olympic athlete of all time. Beginning in 1984 and ending in 2000, Steve won a Rowing gold medal at five Olympic Games in a row. He was 38 when he won his final gold medal.

Wow! That's a boatload of gold medals Steve!

Dame Kelly Holmes (GB)

At the age of 34, Kelly became the first British woman to win two gold medals at the same Olympic Games when she won the 800 metres and 1,500m track races in Athens in 2004.

Michael Phelps (USA)

In 2008, he broke Mark Spitz's record by winning an astonishing eight Olympic Swimming gold medals. He also won six gold medals in 2004. That makes him the most successful Olympic athlete in history.

Usain Bolt (Jamaica)

The tall sprinter became an instant superstar in 2008 by winning gold medals in both the 100 metres and 200m with world-record times. He also won a gold medal in the 4 x100m relay, setting yet another world record.

1996

In Atlanta, American athlete Michael Johnson won gold in both the 200 metres and 400m while wearing golden running shoes!

Paralympic legends

The Paralympic Games always produce amazing performances. Since the first official Games in 1960, many athletes have become world-famous for winning gold medals and breaking records. Here are five of the greatest Paralympians.

I want to be a winner too!

Baroness Tanni Grey-Thompson (GB)

Tanni is one of Britain's best-known Paralympic athletes. She took part in five Paralympic Games between 1988 and 2004 and won 16 wheelchair racing medals, including 11 gold medals.

Trischa Zorn (USA)

Between 1980 and 2004 Trischa won an incredible 41 Paralympic gold medals as a blind swimmer. She is easily the most successful athlete in the history of the Paralympic Games.

2000

Australian athlete Cathy Freeman lit the Olympic Flame to start the Sydney Games. She later won gold in the 400 metres.

Lee Pearson (GB)

Lee has won nine Paralympic gold medals in Dressage. He won three gold medals in 2000, three in 2004 and three in 2008. Can he win another three in London?

David Roberts (GB)

David has won 11 Swimming gold medals at the Paralympic Games. If he wins more in London, he could become Britain's most successful Paralympian of all time.

Oscar Pistorius (South Africa)

Oscar has won four Paralympic gold medals in Athletics. He has set lots of world records and is so fast that he runs as fast as many of the athletes at the Olympic Games.

2000

Rower Steve Redgrave became Britain's most successful ever Olympic athlete when he won his fifth gold medal in five Games.

How to be an Olympian

Being an Olympic athlete takes years of hard work and dedication. World champion diver Tom Daley, who was just 14 when he competed for Team GB at the Beijing 2008 Olympic Games, shares his secrets.

How did you first start diving?

We live by the sea in Plymouth, so my dad wanted to make sure I and my brothers, William and Ben, could swim. There are diving boards next to the swimming pool in Plymouth. I saw other kids diving off them and thought it looked fun. I was seven when I took my first dive.

How many hours a week were you diving to begin with?

At first, one hour a week. When I was eight or nine I was talent-spotted and my training went up to three hours a week.

How often do you train now, and do you enjoy it?

I train 26 hours a week. I love it and I always have done!

Do you have to eat special foods?

I don't have a special diet. I just have to eat sensibly and enough so that I have enough energy to fulfil my training schedule and grow stronger. But I can't eat too much because I need to stay lean.

Do you have your own lucky mascot?

It's not so much a mascot, but I have an orange monkey that I got when I was nine. It comes everywhere with me.

2000

UK wheelchair racer Baroness Tanni Grey-Thompson won four Paralympic gold medals in the 100 metres, 200m, 400m and 800m in Sydney!

What's the best thing about being a diver?
Travelling to different countries, meeting lots of people and training. I really enjoy the trampolining and gymnastics stuff that we have to do.

What is the worst thing?
When you land flat on the water off the boards. It really hurts!

How did you enjoy your first Olympic Games in Beijing?
It was great fun and an incredible experience.

What are your hopes for the Olympic Games in London?
I want to dive the very best I can and, at the very least, win a medal. But I would dearly love to win the gold.

'I would dearly love to win the gold!'

Key Facts

Born: 21 May 1994
Height: 1.62m
Weight: 53kg
Home town: Plymouth
Event: Synchronised and Individual 10-metre Platform Diving

Track Record

2008 Gold medal for 10-metre Platform Diving at the European Championships, Eindhoven
2008 Qualified for the Beijing 2008 Olympic Games in 10m Platform and Synchronised 10m Platform events
2009 Gold medal for 10m Platform Diving at the World Championships in Rome

You have to be totally dedicated to be an Olympian!

2004
The Games returned to Athens, where the ancient Panathenian Stadium was used for Archery and the finish of the Marathon.

It's great that so many people want to get involved!

Behind the scenes

More than 15,000 athletes will compete at the London 2012 Olympic Games and Paralympic Games, but even more people will be working behind the scenes. Thousands of judges, officials and volunteers will help to make the Games run smoothly.

Some of the most important people at the Olympic and Paralympic Games are volunteers. They are people who give up their spare time to help at the Games for free. About 70,000 volunteers will help at the London 2012 Games. Volunteers will do all sorts of jobs, such as checking tickets, organising buses for athletes and showing fans where to go. The Games would not be possible without them, which is why they are also known as Games Makers.

Volunteers, like these at the Beijing 2008 Olympic Games, are easy to spot – they all wear a special uniform.

2004

Dame Kelly Holmes won the 800 metres and 1,500m to become the first British woman to win two gold medals at the same Games.

Safe and sound

As many as 9,000 police officers will be on duty in London on busy days in 2012. There will also be about 5,000 security guards. Keeping the athletes and the public safe is one of the most important jobs during the Games.

The big story

The Olympic Games are the world's largest media event. About 21,000 reporters, photographers and broadcasters will work at the Olympic Games in London. Another 6,500 will work at the Paralympic Games.

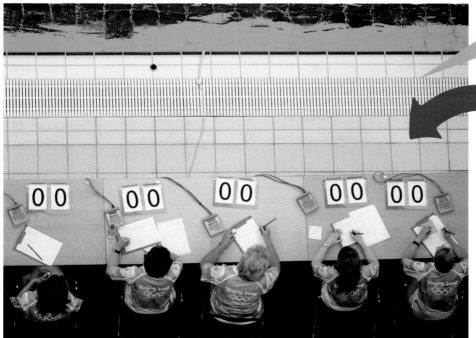

Judges have a very important role to play in sports such as Synchronised Swimming.

Photographers will be on hand to capture the most dramatic moments as they happen!

Live from London!

In London, people covering the Olympic Games for television and radio will work inside a building in the Olympic Park called the International Broadcast Centre. The building is so big that five jumbo jets could easily fit inside it, lined up wing to wing.

2004

China finished top of the medals table at the Paralympic Games with 63 gold medals. Britain came second with 35 golds.

Fun facts!

Did you know that athletes competing at the London 2012 Olympic and Paralympic Games will tuck into 25,000 loaves of bread and 100 tonnes of meat? Here are some big facts about the world's greatest sporting festival!

London 2012 Paralympic Games

- 4,200 .... athletes
- 20 .... sports
- 167 .... countries
- 6,500 .... media and broadcasters
- 2 .... million tickets
- 500 .... gold medals to be won

London 2012 Olympic Games

- 10,500 ..... athletes
- 26 .... sports
- 205 .... countries
- 21,000 ..... media and broadcasters
- 8 .... million tickets
- 302 .... gold medals to be won

Think big!

The Olympic Park in east London is the size of **357** football pitches! Under the park there are **200 kilometres** of electrical cables, which is enough to stretch from London to Nottingham. The main stadium will have **80,000** seats. By the time the Games finish, **one million** spectators will have sat in them.

*The Olympic Stadium was made with **10,000 tonnes** of steel and covers **108,500m²**.*

2005

Britain celebrated when London was chosen to be the host city for the 2012 Olympic Games and Paralympic Games.

Transport for London

London's transport network connects all the different sporting venues around the city.

Spectator statistics

Coping with the huge number of spectators at the Games is a huge challenge for the organisers. On the busiest day, **800,000** fans are expected – that's more than the population of Leeds! Every morning of the Games up to **120,000** visitors will pass through Stratford Regional train station. Trains will arrive at the Olympic Park every 15 seconds.

Snack attack!

Playing sport can make you very hungry. The **14,700** Olympic and Paralympic athletes will munch and slurp their way through...

82 tonnes of seafood
31 tonnes of chicken
100 tonnes of meat
75,000 litres of milk
19 tonnes of eggs
21 tonnes of cheese
330 tonnes of fruit and vegetables

Believe it or not

About **900,000** different items of sports equipment will be needed for the London 2012 Games. That includes **1,424** footballs, **1,111** Badminton shuttlecocks, **8** trampolines and about **65,000** towels!

2008
At the Beijing Games the British team won a total of 19 gold medals, making it the team's best performance for 100 years!

Collectors' corner

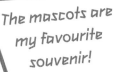

One fun way to enjoy the Olympic Games and Paralympic Games is to collect special souvenirs. From mascots to badges, coins, stamps and toys, there's so much to collect!

The mascots are my favourite souvenir!

Pin mania!

People have collected Olympic badges, or pins as they are also known, since the first modern Games in 1896. Today they are the most popular souvenir to collect. You can buy bright and colourful Olympic and Paralympic pins in shops. Sometimes companies and countries involved in the Games have pins to give away. Lots of people bring their collections to the Games to swap pins with other fans.

Super stamps

Collecting Olympic and Paralympic stamps is also a popular hobby. There are so many stamps to collect because many countries around the world create new stamps every four years to celebrate the Games. The oldest Olympic stamps were made in Greece to celebrate the first Games in 1896. You could start by collecting London 2012 postage stamps.

*Cuddly toy versions of **Wenlock** and **Mandeville** are set to be best-sellers!*

Believe it or not

In 2002, a special Olympic badge was made in America with 89 tiny diamonds. Someone bought it for an incredible £13,000!

2008

Usain Bolt became the fastest man on the planet with world records in the 100 metres and 200m at the Beijing Games.

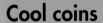

Mascot mad

Mascots are always the most popular souvenirs among children. At the Beijing Games in 2008, there were five cuddly mascots. When they first went on sale, many shops had sold out within hours!

Mandeville visits the official London 2012 shop at King's Cross St Pancras station.

Cool coins

Coin-collecting is another great way to enjoy the Games. Most countries that host the Games produce special coins. In the United Kingdom, coins are made by the Royal Mint. To celebrate the Games, the Royal Mint is producing lots of London 2012 coins, including 50 pence pieces with sporting designs.

Shop 'til you drop!

Lots of different souvenirs will be on sale at the London Games. Among the top souvenirs are London 2012 t-shirts or caps. Souvenir shops will be packed with Olympic and Paralympic Games goodies, such as London 2012 toys, jewellery, bags, posters, glasses, mugs and smaller souvenirs like London 2012 pens and key rings.

2008

Paralympic cyclist Darren Kenny won four gold medals and one silver in Beijing. The GB team won 42 gold medals in total.

Gold medal challenge!

The 2012 Games are coming, but are you fully prepared? Test your knowledge now, by taking the Olympic and Paralympic gold medal challenge. Check your answers and see if you can win the gold!

1 Where were the first modern Olympic Games held in 1896?

2 Which of these four words is not part of the Olympic motto: Faster, Higher, Longer, Stronger?

3 At the London 1908 Olympic Games, where did the Marathon race start?

4 What Olympic and Paralympic sport takes place in a velodrome?

5 Who was only 13 when she won two gold medals for Britain at the 2008 Paralympic Games in Beijing?

6 Aquatics is made up of four water sports. Swimming, Synchronised Swimming, Water Polo and which other?

7 Which British rower won an amazing five Olympic gold medals?

Are you game on to take the challenge?

88

2009
Construction was well underway on all the venues at the Olympic Park in east London, in preparation for the London 2012 Games.

(8) Where did Britain finish in the final medals table at the last Paralympic Games in Beijing?

(9) Which is the odd one out: Boxing, Equestrian, Gymnastics, Motor Racing?

(10) Which swimmer won eight gold medals at the 2008 Olympic Games in Beijing?

Yay! You're going for gold!

(11) Unscramble these letters to find a famous Olympic athlete.... I BAN LOUTS.

(12) Long jump, Pole vault, Triple jump. What other jumping event is part of Athletics?

(13) Olympic and Paralympic gold medals are made out of solid gold. True or false?

(14) What is the only Olympic sport in which men and women compete against each other?

(15) In which sport do competitors cross the finish line backwards?

Answers on page 95.

Medal time!

How did you do in the *gold medal challenge*? Check all your answers on page 95, then find which medal you've won here.

SCORE: 11 or more!
Congratulations! You've just won a shiny **GOLD** medal.

SCORE: 7 to 11
Well done! You've won yourself a super **SILVER** medal!

SCORE: 6 or below
Great effort! You've won the **BRONZE** medal this time.

2010
The organisers of the London Olympic and Paralympic Games invited people to volunteer to become Games Makers in 2012.

Cultural Olympiad

Wow! It's a creative festival too!

The London 2012 Games are not just about sport. Other events involving acting, singing, dancing and art will take place too. All this creative fun is part of the Cultural Olympiad!

The Cultural Olympiad began in 2008 after the Beijing Games and lasts for four years. It includes big events involving famous singers and actors as well as small events in cities, towns and villages across the country. The idea is for everyone, especially children and young people, to join in the fun.

Festival of fun

To mark the Games, a 12-week festival will take place in towns and cities all over the country. It is called The London 2012 Festival and it will run from 21 June until 9 September 2012, the last day of the Paralympic Games. The festival will include famous pop stars, artists, dancers and other performers.

The Cultural Olympiad celebrates creativity all around the country.

Believe it or not

As part of the Cultural Olympiad an artist will create an amazing spinning column of cloud and light that will rise as far as the eye can see from Birkenhead's disused Morpeth dock, directly opposite the city of Liverpool!

2011

An incredible 10 million tickets for the London Olympic Games and Paralympic Games will go on sale to the public.

World of music

A week before the Olympic Games Opening Ceremony there will be a 'River of Music' on the River Thames in London. Famous musicians will perform with young people from all over the world on five big stages on the riverside. The stages will represent the five main continents of the world.

The Cultural Olympiad brings different types of art together too – like hip hop and Shakespeare!

Hugely artistic!

Artists are creating lots of pictures and sculptures for the London 2012 Games. The biggest piece of art is a giant red tower made out of spirals of metal. It will be 118 metres tall – more than twice the height of Nelson's Column in London – and it will tower over the Olympic Park. There will even be a restaurant with amazing views over London at the top. Thankfully you will be able to travel all the way there in a lift!

*This colossal red tower will be created by world-famous sculptor **Anish Kapoor**.*

Word play

Art and performance was also part of the ancient Olympic Games in Greece. Alongside the sporting events there were performances of poetry and rhetoric, which was a type of public-speaking competition.

2012
On 27 July, the Flame will be lit at the Opening Ceremony to mark the start of the London 2012 Olympic Games!

Time to celebrate!

The countdown is complete. On 27 July 2012, the Olympic Games will begin with a dazzling Opening Ceremony and the Olympic Flame will be lit inside London's Olympic Stadium. Let the Games begin...

Let's party!

The Olympic Flame is the signal to start a sporting celebration like no other!

The Opening Ceremony is always spectacular. It begins with the flag of the host country being raised. Then there is an artistic show involving many hundreds of performers. After the show, the athletes from all 205 nations parade into the stadium. The Olympic flag is raised and a runner enters the stadium, carrying the Olympic Torch. The Torch is carried to the Olympic cauldron and the Flame is lit.

Greece is always the first country to enter the stadium for the athletes' parade. This is to honour the ancient Games in Greece. Teams then parade in alphabetical order. By tradition, the host country is the last team to enter the stadium. That means the British team will end the parade in 2012. They are sure to get the biggest cheer from the home crowd.

Believe it or not

Doves used to be released during Opening Ceremonies as a symbol of peace. Birds are not released any more because of what happened at the Opening Ceremony in Seoul in 1988. A few doves perched on the edge of the Olympic cauldron just before it was lit. When the flame was lit, the poor birds were roasted.

2012
The London Olympic Games will come to an end on 12 August, finishing with a spectacular Closing Ceremony.

Torch Bearer

It is great honour to be the final Torch Bearer who lights the Olympic Flame. Usually, the person chosen is a famous athlete, but their name is always kept a secret until the Opening Ceremony. Who will light the Flame in London?

The Paralympic Flame

The Paralympic Games have their own spectacular Opening Ceremony. It is very similar to the ceremony for the Olympic Games and ends with the lighting of the Paralympic cauldron. The Opening Ceremony for the Paralympic Games in London is on 29 August.

Fair play

During the Opening Ceremonies for the Olympic Games and Paralympic Games, an athlete takes an oath on behalf of all the other athletes taking part. The athlete promises to obey the rules, respect their opponents and to not cheat in any way. A judge also makes a promise on behalf of the rest of the judges to be fair to all the athletes.

The Closing Ceremony is every bit as colourful and exciting as the Opening Ceremony. Prepare for the wow-factor!

2012

The London Paralympic Games will open on 29 August lasting until the Closing Ceremony on 9 September.

And beyond...

After weeks of incredible sport, the Olympic Games and Paralympic Games will end with two Closing Ceremonies. Athletes will leave with new friendships and amazing memories.

Hooray! The Olympic Games forever!

Like the Opening Ceremonies, the Closing Ceremonies are a mixture of speeches and spectacular displays by performers. They include a parade of athletes, but this time the athletes enter the stadium together and not in their teams. To show that the Games are over, the Olympic and Paralympic Flames are finally put out.

During the Closing Ceremonies, the host country of the next Games has the honour of performing a short show. In Beijing, it was London's turn to perform. This time it will be Rio de Janeiro, the second largest city in Brazil.

Athletes enter the stadium for the Closing Ceremony in one big, friendly group.

2016
The Olympic dream continues! Fast forward to the 31st Olympic Games, which will open in Rio de Janeiro.